SCHOLASTIC

Writing Lessons to Meet the Common Core

Grade 6

Linda Ward Beech

NEW YORK ● TORONTO ● LONDON ● AUCKLAND ● SYDNEY
MEXICO CITY ● NEW DELHI ● HONG KONG ● BUENOS AIRES

Cover design by Scott Davis
Interior design by Kathy Massaro
Image credits: page 39 (left) © Andreas Meyer/Big Stock Photo, (right) © Corey Ford/Big Stock Photo; page 42 © iStockphoto.com/powerofforever. All images © 2013.
Illustrations by ALAN126, Teresa Anderko, Constanza Basaluzzo, Hector Borlasca, Maxie Chambliss, Rusty Fletcher, Aleksey and Olga Ivanov

ISBN: 978-0-545-49600-1

1 2 3 4 5 6 7 8 9 10   40   20 19 18 17 16 15 14 13

Contents

About This Book

. . . .

To build a foundation for college and career readiness, students need to learn to use writing as a way of offering and supporting opinions, demonstrating understanding of the subjects they are studying, and conveying real and imagined experiences and events. They learn to appreciate that a key purpose of writing is to communicate clearly to an external, sometimes unfamiliar audience, and they begin to adapt the form and content of their writing to accomplish a particular task and purpose.

—COMMON CORE STATE STANDARDS FOR ENGLISH LANGUAGE ARTS, JUNE 2010

This book includes step-by-step instructions for teaching the three forms of writing—Argument, Informative/Explanatory, and Narrative—covered in the Common Core State Standards (CCSS). The CCSS are a result of a state-led effort to establish a single set of clear educational standards aimed at providing students nationwide with a high-quality education. The standards outline the knowledge and skills that students should achieve during their years in school.

The writing standards are a subset of the Common Core English Language Arts Standards. They provide "a focus for instruction" to help students gain a mastery of a range of skills and applications necessary for writing clear prose. This book is divided into three main sections; each section includes six lessons devoted to one of the writing forms covered in the CCSS for grade 6. You'll find more about each of these types of writing on pages 6–7.

- **Lessons 1–6** (pages 8–25) focus on the standards for writing arguments.
- **Lessons 7–12** (pages 26–43) emphasize standards particular to informative/explanatory writing. (Lesson 7 focuses on the important skill of summarizing and paraphrasing information in research notes.)
- **Lessons 13–18** (pages 44–61) address the standards for narrative writing.

Although the CCSS do not specify how to teach any form of writing, the lessons in this book follow the gradual release of responsibility model of instruction: I Do It, We Do It, You Do It (Pearson & Gallagher, 1983). This model provides educators with a framework for releasing responsibility to students in a gradual manner. It recognizes that we learn best when a concept is demonstrated to us; when we have sufficient time to practice it with support; and when we are then given the opportunity to try it on our own. Each phase is equally important, but the chief goal is to teach for independence—the You Do It phase—so that students really learn to take over the skill and apply it in new situations.

Pearson, P. D., & Gallagher, M. C. (1983). "The Instruction of Reading Comprehension." *Contemporary Educational Psychology*, 8 (3).

A Look at the Lessons

The lessons in each section progress in difficulty and increase in the number of objectives and standards covered. This format enables you to use beginning or later lessons in a section depending on your students' abilities. Each lesson begins with a list of the objectives and standards. A general reproducible assessment checklist of standards for each writing form appears at the end of the book. (See pages 62–64.)

Here's a look at the features in each lesson.

Lesson Page 1

The first page is the teaching page of each lesson. It provides a step-by-step plan for using the student reproducible on the second lesson page and the On Your Own activity on the third lesson page. The teaching page closely follows the organization of the student reproducibles. This page also models sample text that students might generate when completing page 2 of the lesson. Finally, the teaching page includes an opportunity for students to review their classmates' work using the reproducible assessment checklist customized to the lesson's writing form. Each checklist also reminds students to check for correct spelling, punctuation, and paragraph form.

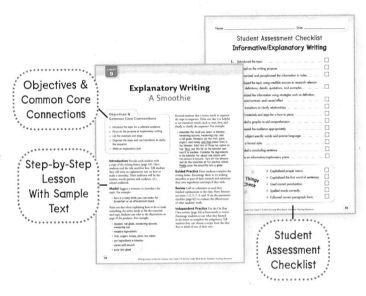

Objectives & Common Core Connections

Step-by-Step Lesson With Sample Text

Student Assessment Checklist

Lesson Page 2

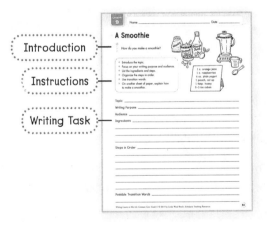

Introduction

Instructions

Writing Task

The second page is a student reproducible, which is the core of the lesson. Students complete this writing frame as you guide them. In most lessons, students use the completed page as the basis for a text they write on a separate sheet of paper.

Although you provide a model for completing this reproducible, you'll want to encourage students to use their own ideas, words, and sentences as much as possible.

Lesson Page 3

The third page is a writing frame for independent work. It follows a format similar to the one students used for the first reproducible. Students choose their topic from the suggested list or use their own idea. In most lessons, students use the completed page as the basis for a text they write on a separate sheet of paper.

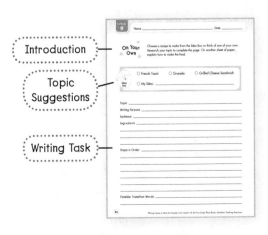

Introduction

Topic Suggestions

Writing Task

Three Forms of Writing

The CCSS focus on three forms of writing—argument, informative/explanatory, and narrative. In grade 6, students are expected to learn to "establish and maintain a formal style" in both argument and informative/explanatory pieces.

Argument Pieces (Standards W.6.1, W.6.1a, W.6.1b, W.6.1c, W.6.1d, W.6.1e)

The purpose of writing an argument is to support a claim and/or to convince others to think or act in a certain way, to encourage readers or listeners to share the writer's opinion, beliefs, or position. Argument pieces are also known as persuasive writing.

> Coin collecting, or numismatics, is an absorbing and worthy hobby.

In developing an argument, students must learn to make a claim and supply valid reasons, facts, and expert opinions to support it. Phrases such as *I think*, *the facts show*, and *the evidence shows* all signal arguments.

> A baseball glove will give people of the future a good sense of American culture.

When teaching these lessons, display different examples of arguments. You might include:

- essays
- editorials
- book, movie, TV, and theater reviews
- print advertisements
- letters of appeal
- letters to the editor
- feature columns

> As students learn to produce different forms of writing, they are also enhancing their ability to recognize these forms in their reading.

Informative/Explanatory Writing (Standards W.6.2, W.6.2a, W.6.2b, W.6.2c, W.6.2d, W.6.2e, W.6.2f)

The purpose of informative/explanatory writing is to inform the reader by giving facts and by conveying ideas, concepts, explanations, and other information. Informative/explanatory writing is also called expository writing.

When writing an informative/explanatory piece, students must introduce the topic and give facts, details, descriptions, analysis, and other information about the topic. The information should be organized in a logical way. Many kinds of informative/explanatory writing require research. Sometimes illustrations are included with informative/explanatory pieces.

> A sneeze is a reflex action of muscles to remove an irritation in the nose.

Display different examples of informative/explanatory writing. You might include:

- reports
- news articles
- how-to articles
- biographies
- directions
- textbooks
- magazines
- recipes

> Conduct a mini-lesson on reliable sources when students are working on argument or informative writing. Provide examples of reliable references and websites.

Writing Lessons to Meet the Common Core: Grade 6 © 2013 by Linda Ward Beech, Scholastic Teaching Resources

Narrative Writing (Standards W.6.3, W.6.3a, W.6.3b, W.6.3c, W.6.3d, W.6.3e)

The purpose of narrative writing is to entertain. A narrative gives an account or a story. Usually, a narrative tells about something that happens over a period of time. Narratives can be true or imaginary.

Sally would never forget the day when time went backwards.

When working on a narrative, students must develop a real or imagined experience or event. They must also establish a situation, or plot and setting, create characters, and recount events in a chronological sequence. Narratives usually include descriptive details. Many include dialogue to show the feelings of characters and how they respond to events.

"This recipe sure has a lot of ingredients," said Dad as he emptied his grocery bags.

When introducing narrative writing, display different examples. You might include:

- stories
- mysteries
- fables
- folktales
- myths
- science fiction
- friendly letters

Additional Writing Standards

Although this book focuses on the forms of writing called for in the CCSS, you can also incorporate the standards that relate to the production and distribution of writing and research to build and present knowledge. These standards include:

- W.6.4 Produce writing in which the development and organization are appropriate to task and purpose.

- W.6.5 Develop and strengthen writing as needed by planning, revising, and editing.

- W.6.6 Use technology to produce and publish writing and to interact with others; use keyboarding skills.

- W.6.7 Conduct short research projects drawing on several sources.

- W.6.8 Gather information from multiple print and digital sources. Assess the credibility of each source. Quote or paraphrase the data while avoiding plagiarism and provide bibliographic information for sources.

- W.6.9 Draw evidence from informational texts to support analysis, reflection, and research.

- W.6.10 Write routinely over extended time frames allowing for research, reflection, and revision.

Language Standards

You can also incorporate the CCSS Language Standards that focus on the conventions of standard English grammar and usage when writing or speaking (L.6.1); the conventions of standard English capitalization, punctuation, and spelling when writing (L.6.2); and the knowledge of language and conventions when writing, speaking, reading, or listening (L.6.3).

Writing Lessons to Meet the Common Core: Grade 6 © 2013 by Linda Ward Beech, Scholastic Teaching Resources

Argument Writing
Worthwhile Week

Objectives & Common Core Connections

* Introduce a claim.
* Focus on the purpose of writing an argument.
* Support the claim with clear reasons.
* Organize the information.
* Write an argument.

Introduction Provide each student with a copy of the writing frame (page 9). Have students read the title and first line. Ask students to choose the week they think would be better for the class to observe. Explain that they will be writing an argument to persuade others to support the week they choose. Point out that students might need to do research. Have appropriate reference materials and a computer with Internet access available for student research. Students will also need to use these during the Independent Practice activity.

Model Tell students that when you write an argument, you first introduce the claim or statement of what you think is right, true, best, and so on. For example:

* The class would benefit greatly by observing Geography Awareness Week.

Emphasize that the purpose of writing an argument is to persuade others to agree with your point of view. Ask: *How do you persuade someone to agree with you?* Help students understand that a writer should give clear reasons to support a claim. Suggest some reasons that might support celebrating Geography Awareness Week. For example:

* better understand place where we live
* responsibility to planet and people
* diversity of people and cultures
* how resources shape life

Coach students in organizing the information and then developing it into complete sentences. For example, the first three sentences below relate to things students can learn from geography while the last sentence focuses on their own role as global citizens.

* Geography helps us better understand the locality and region in which we live.
* It helps us appreciate the diversity of people and cultures in the world.
* It teaches us how natural resources shape life on earth.
* Geography also inspires us to think about our own responsibility to the planet and the people on it.

Guided Practice Have students complete the writing frame. Encourage them to use their own reasons, wording, and sentence structure. If students choose to argue for Be Kind to Animals Week, guide them in developing reasons to support their claim.

Review Call on volunteers to read their finished arguments to the class. Have listeners use items 1–4 and 9 on the assessment checklist (page 62) to evaluate the effectiveness of other students' work.

Independent Practice Use the On Your Own activity (page 10) as homework or review. Encourage students to use what they learned in the lesson to complete the assignment. Explain that students can choose a week from the Idea Box or research one of their own.

Writing Lessons to Meet the Common Core: Grade 6 © 2013 by Linda Ward Beech, Scholastic Teaching Resources

Worthwhile Week

Which would be the better week to observe?

- Introduce a claim.
- Focus on the purpose of writing an argument.
- Support the claim with reasons.
- Organize the information.
- Write an argument on another sheet of paper.

Claim _____

_____

Writing Purpose _____

_____

Supporting Reasons _____

_____

_____

_____

Organizing Information

Group 1 _____

_____

_____

_____

Group 2 _____

_____

_____

On Your Own

Which of these weeks do you think your class should observe?
Choose a week from the Idea Box or research one of your own.
Complete the page. Then, write your argument on another sheet of paper.

Idea Box

○ National School Lunch Week   ○ My Idea: _____

○ American Education Week   _____

○ Fire Prevention Week   _____

Claim _____

_____

Writing Purpose _____

_____

Supporting Reasons _____

_____

_____

_____

_____

Organizing Information

Group 1 _____

_____

_____

_____

Group 2 _____

_____

Argument Writing
Hobby Talk

Objectives & Common Core Connections

* Introduce a claim.
* Focus on the purpose of writing an argument.
* Focus on the audience.
* Support the claim with relevant reasons.
* Organize the information.
* Write an argument.

Introduction Provide each student with a copy of the writing frame (page 12). Have students read the title and first line. Ask students to choose the hobby they think would be more interesting. Explain that they will be writing an argument to support their claim. Their audience will be other class members. Point out that students might need to do research. Have appropriate reference materials and a computer with Internet access available for student research. Students will also need to use these during the Independent Practice activity.

Model Remind students that when you write an argument, you first introduce the claim or statement of what you think is right, true, best, and so on. For example:

* Coin collecting, or numismatics, is an absorbing and worthy hobby.

Review that the purpose of writing an argument is to persuade others to agree with your point of view. Discuss reasons that a writer might give for the claim about coin collecting. For example:

* works of art
* investment
* famous people and events
* historical significance

Coach students in organizing the information and then developing it into complete sentences. For example, the supporting reasons might be organized according to their importance.

* For some people, a collection of rare coins is an investment that can later be sold for a profit.
* Some collectors research and acquire coins of historical significance.
* Coins from ancient civilizations are often beautifully made works of art.
* Collectors can learn about famous people and events through coins.

Guided Practice Have students complete the writing frame. Encourage them to use their own reasons, wording, and sentence structure. If students choose to argue for autographs as a hobby, guide them in developing reasons to support their claim.

Review Call on volunteers to read their finished arguments to the class. Have listeners use items 1–5 and 9 on the assessment checklist (page 62) to evaluate the effectiveness of other students' work.

Independent Practice Use the On Your Own activity (page 13) as homework or review. Encourage students to use what they learned in the lesson to complete the assignment. Explain that students can choose a hobby from the Idea Box or select one of their own.

Writing Lessons to Meet the Common Core: Grade 6 © 2013 by Linda Ward Beech, Scholastic Teaching Resources

Name _____ Date _____

Hobby Talk

Which would be the more interesting hobby to pursue?

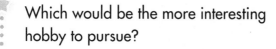

Collecting Autographs

Numismatics (Coin Collecting)

- Introduce a claim.
- Focus on the purpose of writing an argument.
- Think about your audience.
- Support the claim with reasons.
- Organize the information.
- Write an argument on another sheet of paper.

Claim _____

_____

Writing Purpose _____

_____

Audience _____

Supporting Reasons _____

_____

_____

_____

Organizing Information

Most Important _____

_____

_____

_____

Least Important _____

_____

_____

On Your Own

Choose a hobby to support from the Idea Box or think of one of your own. Complete the page. Then, write your argument on another sheet of paper.

Idea Box

○ Stamps   ○ Seashells   ○ Postcards

○ My Idea: _____

Claim _____

_____

Writing Purpose _____

_____

Audience _____

Supporting Reasons _____

_____

_____

_____

Organizing Information

Most Important _____

_____

_____

_____

Least Important _____

_____

_____

Argument Writing
Learn a Language

Objectives & Common Core Connections

* Introduce a claim.
* Focus on the writing purpose.
* Focus on the audience.
* Support the claim with evidence from reliable sources.
* Organize the information.
* Write an argument.

Introduction Provide each student with a copy of the writing frame (page 15). Have students read the title and first line. Ask students to choose which language they think would be useful to learn. Explain that they will be writing an argument to support their claim. Their audience will be a committee on school curriculum. Point out that students might need to do research. Have appropriate reference materials and a computer with Internet access available for student research. Students will also need to use these during the Independent Practice activity.

Model Remind students that when you write an argument, you first introduce the claim or statement of what you think is right, true, best, and so on. For example:

* Spanish would be a useful language to learn.

Review that the purpose of writing an argument is to persuade others to agree with your point of view. Suggest reasons that a writer might give for becoming fluent in Spanish. Stress that when you cite reasons or evidence to support an argument, your sources should be reliable. Point out that one source you can use is the U.S. government census website. For example:

* 16.3% of U.S. population is Hispanic
* important for workers in Spanish communities
* useful in careers in diplomacy
* helpful for travel in Latin America

Coach students in organizing the information and then developing it into complete sentences. For example, the first two sentences below relate to Spanish in the U.S., and the last two sentences relate to uses of Spanish in other parts of the world.

* More than 16 percent of the U.S. population is Hispanic, so Spanish words for such things as foods, dances, and styles are becoming more common. Knowing Spanish would be useful for medical personnel, firefighters, teachers, and other kinds of workers in cities with large Hispanic communities.
* Understanding Spanish would be important for a career in diplomacy, especially in Latin America. Spanish would also be helpful for travelers to Latin American countries.

Guided Practice Have students complete the writing frame. Encourage them to use their own reasons, wording, and sentence structure. If students choose to argue for learning Mandarin, guide them in developing evidence to support their claim. (Note: For ELL students, you might suggest they choose English.)

Review Call on volunteers to read their finished arguments to the class. Have listeners use items 1–5 and 9 on the assessment checklist (page 62) to evaluate the effectiveness of other students' work.

Independent Practice Use the On Your Own activity (page 16) as homework or review. Encourage students to use what they learned in the lesson to complete the assignment. Explain that students can choose a language from the Idea Box or select one of their own.

Name _____ Date _____

Learn a Language

Which would be more useful to learn as a second language?

- Introduce a claim.
- Focus on the purpose of writing an argument.
- Think about your audience.
- Support the claim with evidence.
- Organize the information.
- Write an argument on another sheet of paper.

Claim _____

_____

Writing Purpose _____

_____

Audience _____

Supporting Evidence _____

_____

_____

_____

Organizing Information

Group 1 _____

_____

_____

_____

Group 2 _____

_____

_____

Name _____ Date _____

On Your Own

Choose another language to learn from the Idea Box or think of one of your own. Complete the page. Then, write your argument on another sheet of paper.

Idea Box

○ Arabic   ○ Urdu   ○ Russian

○ My Idea: _____

Claim _____

_____

Writing Purpose _____

_____

Audience _____

Supporting Evidence _____

_____

_____

_____

Organizing Information

Group 1 _____

_____

_____

_____

Group 2 _____

_____

_____

Argument Writing
Time Capsule

Objectives & Common Core Connections

* Introduce a claim.
* Focus on the writing purpose and audience.
* Support the claim with relevant evidence.
* Use words to clarify relationships.
* Organize the information.
* Write an argument.

Introduction Provide each student with a copy of the writing frame (page 18). Have students read the title and first lines. Ask students to think about what they would include in a time capsule. Explain that they will be writing an argument to support their claim. Their audience will be other class members.

Model Tell students that you have chosen to include a baseball glove. Remind them that when you write an argument, you first introduce the claim or statement of what you think is right, true, best, and so on. For example:

* A baseball glove will give people of the future a sense of American culture.

Stress that when you cite reasons or evidence to support an argument, your evidence should be relevant to your argument. Invite students to suggest reasons or researched evidence that would support the claim above. For example:

* sports as popular pastime
* competitive
* specialized equipment
* concerned with safety
* protective equipment
* played with ball

Coach students in developing the reasons into complete sentences. Model how to use words, such as *since* and *also*, and phrases to clarify the relationship between the claim and evidence. Guide students in organizing the information. In this case, the first sentences relate to sports in general, while the other sentences relate to the baseball glove. For example:

* A piece of sporting equipment suggests that sports are a popular American pastime in the 21st century. <u>Since</u> sports are competitive, the glove tells you that Americans like to compete.

* The glove is slightly cup-shaped, which indicates that it is meant to hold or catch something such as a ball. This attention to design suggests that Americans use specialized equipment for their sports. The glove is <u>also</u> made of thick, protective leather, which suggests that Americans are concerned with safety.

Guided Practice Have students complete the writing frame. Encourage them to use their own reasons, wording, and sentence structure.

Review Call on volunteers to read their finished arguments to the class. Have listeners use items 1–6 and 9 on the assessment checklist (page 62) to evaluate the effectiveness of other students' work.

Independent Practice Use the On Your Own activity (page 19) as homework or review. Encourage students to use what they learned in the lesson to complete the assignment. Explain that students can choose a piece of sports equipment from the Idea Box or select one of their own.

Name _____ Date _____

Time Capsule

Your class is putting together a time capsule to be opened in 100 years. Each student can choose one item to include. What do you choose?

- Introduce a claim.
- Think about your writing purpose and audience.
- Support the claim with evidence.
- Use words to clarify relationships.
- Organize the information.
- Write an argument on another sheet of paper.

Claim _____

_____

Purpose/Audience _____

_____

Supporting Evidence _____

_____

_____

_____

Possible Clarifying Words _____

_____

Organizing Information

Group 1 _____

_____

_____

_____

Group 2 _____

_____

Writing Lessons to Meet the Common Core: Grade 6 © 2013 by Linda Ward Beech, Scholastic Teaching Resources

Name _____ Date _____

On Your Own

Choose a piece of sports equipment for a time capsule from the Idea Box or think of one of your own. Complete the page. Then, write your argument on another sheet of paper.

Idea Box

○ Lacrosse Stick   ○ Football Helmet   ○ Soccer Ball

○ My Idea: _____

Claim _____

_____

Purpose/Audience _____

_____

Supporting Evidence _____

_____

_____

_____

Possible Clarifying Words _____

_____

Organizing Information

Group 1 _____

_____

_____

_____

Group 2 _____

_____

Argument Writing
Snack Machines

Objectives & Common Core Connections

✳ Introduce a claim.

✳ Focus on the writing purpose and audience.

✳ Support the claim with relevant evidence.

✳ Use words to clarify relationships.

✳ Organize the information.

✳ Write an argument in a formal style.

Introduction Provide each student with a copy of the writing frame (page 21). Have students read the title and first line. Ask students to think about what their position on this topic is. Explain that they will be writing an argument to support their claim. Their audience will be the school board.

Model Tell students that you will use a formal writing style for this audience. Say: *In a formal style you avoid contractions, abbreviations, and slang. You write in the third person, using a tone that is polite but impersonal.* Point out that a formal style is often used in reports. Suggest a sentence to introduce a claim. For example:

- Vending machines with healthy snacks would have a positive impact on middle schools.

Remind students that when you cite reasons or evidence to support an argument, the evidence should be relevant or strongly related to the argument. Invite students to suggest or find evidence that would support the claim above. For example:

- convenient
- provide energy
- good nutrition
- replace unhealthful snacks
- great for students with late lunch hours

Coach students in developing the reasons into complete sentences. Model how to use words and phrases to clarify the relationship between the claim and evidence. Guide students in organizing the information. The first two sentences below relate to the nutritious value of healthful snacks, while the last two sentences focus on the convenience for students. For example:

- Healthful snacks would offer nutritious food to students; furthermore, these snacks would replace the junk food that students so often eat. Healthy snacks would also be a good source of energy for students throughout the day.

- The vending machines would be a convenient way for students to get snacks. Moreover, these machines would be particularly useful to students who don't eat any or enough breakfast and are scheduled for late lunches.

Guided Practice Have students complete the writing frame. Encourage them to use their own reasons, wording, and sentence structure. If students choose to argue against vending machines, guide them in developing evidence to support their claim.

Review Call on volunteers to read their finished arguments to the class. Have listeners use items 1–7 and 9 on the assessment checklist (page 62) to evaluate the effectiveness of other students' work.

Independent Practice Use the On Your Own activity (page 22) as homework or review. Encourage students to use what they learned in the lesson to complete the assignment. Explain that students can choose a class from the Idea Box or select one of their own.

Name _____ Date _____

Snack Machines

Should middle schools have vending machines with healthful snacks?

- Introduce a claim.
- Think about your writing purpose and audience.
- Support the claim with evidence and use words to clarify relationships.
- Organize the information.
- Write an argument in a formal style on another sheet of paper.

Claim _____

_____

Purpose/Audience _____

Supporting Evidence _____

_____

_____

_____

Possible Clarifying Words _____

Organizing Information

Group 1 _____

_____

_____

Group 2 _____

_____

_____

On Your Own

Choose a class that you think middle schools should have from the Idea Box or think of one of your own. Complete the page. Then, write a formal argument on another sheet of paper.

Idea Box

○ Cooking Class   ○ Nutrition Class   ○ Fitness Class

○ My Idea: _____

Claim _____

_____

Purpose/Audience _____

Supporting Evidence _____

_____

_____

_____

Possible Clarifying Words _____

Organizing Information

Group 1 _____

_____

_____

Group 2 _____

_____

_____

Argument Writing
School Uniforms

Objectives & Common Core Connections

* Introduce a claim.
* Focus on writing purpose and audience.
* Support the claim with relevant evidence.
* Organize the information and use words to clarify relationships.
* Write a concluding statement.
* Write an argument in a formal style.

Introduction Provide each student with a copy of the writing frame (page 24). Have students read the title and first line. Ask students to think about what their position on this topic is. Explain that they will be writing an argument to support their claim. Their audience will be readers of a local newspaper.

Model Tell students that you will use a formal writing style for this audience. Say: *In a formal style you avoid contractions, abbreviations, and slang. You write in the third person, using a tone that is polite but impersonal.* Suggest a sentence to introduce a claim. For example:

* Students would benefit from wearing school uniforms.

Invite students to suggest or find evidence that would support this claim. For example:

* sense of belonging
* create equality
* cheaper than wearing different outfits
* sign of school spirit
* eliminate morning clothing decisions
* develop sense of pride and responsibility

Coach students in developing the reasons into complete sentences. Model how to use words and phrases to clarify the relationship between the claim and evidence. Guide students in organizing the information. The first three sentences below relate to intangible benefits, while the last two sentences focus on more practical considerations. For example:

* Wearing uniforms creates a sense of belonging and equality among students. Consequently, uniforms can help foster a strong school spirit. As students experience feelings of pride, they also develop a sense of responsibility.

* Wearing a school uniform has practical benefits too; for example, it eliminates the often agonizing task of deciding what to wear each morning. Furthermore, it is less expensive to buy uniforms than to constantly buy the latest clothing fads.

Explain that an argument should have a concluding sentence to restate the writer's claim. For example:

* Clearly, school uniforms have many advantages for students.

Guided Practice Have students complete the writing frame. Encourage them to use their own reasons, wording, and sentences. If students choose to argue against uniforms, guide them in developing evidence to support their claim.

Review Call on volunteers to read their finished arguments to the class. Have listeners use items 1–9 on the assessment checklist (page 62) to evaluate the effectiveness of other students' work.

Independent Practice Use the On Your Own activity (page 25) as homework or review. Encourage students to use what they learned in the lesson to complete the assignment. Explain that students can choose a program from the Idea Box or select one of their own.

School Uniforms

Students should wear school uniforms.

- Introduce a claim.
- Focus on your writing purpose and audience.
- Support the claim with evidence.
- Organize information, use words to clarify relationships, and write a concluding statement.
- Write an argument in a formal style on another sheet of paper.

Claim _____

_____

Purpose/Audience _____

Supporting Evidence _____

_____

_____

_____

Possible Clarifying Words _____

Organizing Information

Group 1 _____

_____

_____

Group 2 _____

_____

_____

_____

_____

Concluding Statement _____

_____

Name _____ Date _____

On Your Own

Choose a program that you think schools should have from the Idea Box or think of one of your own. Complete the page. Then, write a formal argument on another sheet of paper.

Idea Box

○ Dress Code   ○ Required Community Service   ○ Mentor Program

○ My Idea: _____

Claim _____

_____

Purpose/Audience _____

Supporting Evidence _____

_____

_____

_____

Possible Clarifying Words _____

Organizing Information

   Group 1 _____

_____

_____

   Group 2 _____

_____

_____

_____

Concluding Statement _____

Informative Writing
The Unicorn

Objectives & Common Core Connections

* Focus on the topic.
* Focus on purpose of informative writing.
* Conduct research using reliable sources.
* Summarize or paraphrase information in notes.

Introduction Provide each student with a copy of the writing frame (page 27). Have students read the title and first line. Tell them that they will develop facts for a paragraph about the unicorn. Point out that the purpose of informative writing is to inform or educate readers. Explain that it is necessary to do research for this kind of writing. Have available appropriate reference materials and a computer with Internet access. Students will also need to use these during the Independent Practice activity.

Model Say: *The topic is unicorns.* Point out that although the sample text on page 27 gives some information about this topic, writers can't simply copy it. Stress that when students do research, they must take notes and paraphrase the information by putting it in their own words. Suggest that students look for key words such as *imaginary creature, art forms,* and *attributes* before taking notes. For example:

* imaginary creature—one horn, looks like white horse
* art forms—literature, mosaics, frescoes, tapestries, paintings
* attributes—religious, secular, magical, medicinal

Coach students in developing sentences from their notes. For example:

* According to legends, the unicorn is an animal resembling a horse with a long horn that projects from its head. This imaginary creature has been portrayed in literature and many works of art, including tapestries, frescoes, mosaics, and paintings. Beliefs about the unicorn range from religious interpretations to magical powers to medical remedies.

Direct students to use the resources you have assembled to find examples of real animals that people could have mistaken for unicorns and to find examples of literature in which unicorns appear. Have students record notes. For example:

* real animals—narwhal, oryx, eland, aurochs
* literature—Bible, *Julius Caesar* by William Shakespeare, *Harry Potter and the Sorcerer's Stone* by J.K. Rowling

Guided Practice Have students complete the writing frame. Encourage them to use their own wording and sentence structure.

Review Call on volunteers to read their notes, sentences, and research to the class. Have listeners use items 1–4 on the assessment checklist (page 63) to evaluate the effectiveness of other students' work.

Independent Practice Use the On Your Own activity (page 28) as homework or review. Encourage students to use what they learned in the lesson to complete the assignment. Students can choose an imaginary creature from the Idea Box or think of one of their own.

The Unicorn

What is a unicorn?

- Name the topic.
- Focus on your writing purpose.
- Look for key words.
- Take notes in your own words.
- Write practice sentences from your notes.
- Do research on your own. Find examples of real animals that people might have thought were unicorns and of literary works in which unicorns are mentioned.

Topic _____

Writing Purpose _____

Sample Text:

The unicorn is an imaginary creature that looks like a white horse with a single large horn extending from its forehead. Since antiquity, the unicorn has appeared throughout the world in literature, mosaics, frescoes, tapestries, paintings, and other art forms. Because various attributes, both religious and secular, have been assigned to it, the unicorn has long been a subject of intense fascination. In the past, many people believed that the unicorn's horn contained magical and medicinal properties.

Key Words _____

_____

Practice Notes _____

_____

_____

Practice Sentences _____

_____

_____

_____

Research and Notes _____

_____

_____

_____

_____

_____

_____

Name _____ Date _____

On Your Own

Choose an imaginary creature from the Idea Box or think of your own. Research your topic to complete the page.

Idea Box

○ Elf   ○ Dragon   ○ Giant

○ My Idea: _____

Topic _____

Writing Purpose _____

Key Words _____

Research and Notes _____

_____

_____

_____

_____

_____

_____

_____

Practice Sentences _____

_____

_____

_____

_____

Informative Writing
A Sneeze

Objectives & Common Core Connections

* Introduce the topic for a selected audience.
* Focus on the purpose of informative writing.
* Develop the topic with researched, relevant facts.
* Use a cause-and-effect organization.
* Write an informative text.

Introduction Provide each student with a copy of the writing frame (page 30). Have students read the title and first line. Tell students that they will write an informative text explaining why people sneeze. Their audience will be a sixth grade science class. Remind students that the purpose of this kind of writing is to educate the reader. It is usually necessary to do research for informative writing. Have available appropriate reference materials and a computer with Internet access. Students will also need to use these during the Independent Practice activity.

Model To introduce the topic, suggest a sentence that defines what a sneeze is. For example:

* A sneeze is a reflexive action of muscles to remove an irritation in the nose.

Help students assemble facts to develop the topic. For example:

* causes—cold, allergy, flu, bright light
* foreign items—dust, pepper, pollen, pet dander
* expelling air
* many muscles
* eyes close

Coach students in developing the information into complete sentences and organizing it into cause-and-effect paragraphs. The first paragraph below discusses causes for sneezes, and the second paragraph tells what happens as a result of a sneeze. For example:

* Sneezes are caused by colds, allergies, the flu, or even bright lights. Foreign items such as dust, pepper, pollen, and pet dander can also bring on a sneeze.
* When someone sneezes, muscles in the chest, abdomen, diaphragm, and vocal cords are involved. The sneezer's eyes close, and tiny particles burst from the nose at a very high speed.

Guided Practice Have students complete the writing frame. Encourage them to use their own research, wording, and sentence structure.

Review Call on volunteers to read their finished pieces to the class. Have listeners use items 1, 2, 4, 5, 9, and 13 on the assessment checklist (page 63) to evaluate the effectiveness of other students' work.

Independent Practice Use the On Your Own activity (page 31) as homework or review. Encourage students to use what they know about taking notes (see Lesson 7) when researching and writing an informative text. Explain that students can choose an involuntary action from the Idea Box or use one of their own. Remind them to use reliable sources and relevant facts for their research.

Name _____ Date _____

A Sneeze

What is a sneeze?

- Introduce the topic.
- Focus on your writing purpose and audience.
- Develop the topic with researched facts.
- Use a cause-and-effect organization.
- On another sheet of paper, write an informative text to define a sneeze.

Topic _____

Writing Purpose _____

_____

Audience _____

Facts _____

_____

_____

_____

Organizing Information

  Causes _____

_____

_____

_____

  Effects _____

_____

_____

_____

Name _____ Date _____

On Your Own

Choose a reflexive action from the Idea Box or think of one of your own. Research your topic to complete the page. Then, write an informative text on another sheet of paper.

Idea Box

○ Blink   ○ Snore   ○ Hiccup

○ My Idea: _____

Topic _____

Writing Purpose _____

_____

Audience _____

Facts _____

_____

_____

_____

Organizing Information

Causes _____

_____

_____

_____

Effects _____

_____

_____

_____

Explanatory Writing
A Smoothie

Objectives & Common Core Connections

* Introduce the topic for a selected audience.
* Focus on the purpose of explanatory writing.
* List the materials and steps.
* Organize the steps and use transitions to clarify the sequence.
* Write an explanatory text.

Introduction Provide each student with a copy of the writing frame (page 33). Have students read the title and first line. Tell students they will write an explanatory text on how to make a smoothie. Their audience will be the readers, mostly parents and students, of a school cookbook.

Model Suggest a sentence to introduce the topic. For example:

* Here is a tasty drink you can make for breakfast or an afterschool snack.

Point out that when explaining how to do or make something, the writer needs to list the materials and steps. Students can refer to the illustrations on page 33 for guidance. For example:

* blender, tall glass, measuring spoons, measuring cup
* measure ingredients
* fruit, yogurt, honey, juice, ice cubes
* put ingredients in blender
* puree until smooth
* pour into glass

Remind students that a writer needs to organize the steps in sequence. Point out that it is helpful to use transition words, such as *next, then,* and *finally,* to clarify the sequence. For example:

* Assemble the tools you need: a blender, measuring spoons, measuring cup, and a tall glass. Measure out the fruit, juice, yogurt, and honey <u>and then</u> place them in the blender. Add two or three ice cubes on top. <u>Next</u>, put the lid on the blender and turn it to medium. Combine the ingredients in the blender for about one minute until the mixture is smooth. Turn off the blender and let the smoothie sit for another minute. <u>Finally</u>, pour the smoothie into a glass.

Guided Practice Have students complete the writing frame. Encourage them to try making smoothies as part of their research and substitute their own ingredients and steps if they wish.

Review Call on volunteers to read their finished explanations to the class. Have listeners use items 1–2, 5–7, 9, and 13 on the assessment checklist (page 63) to evaluate the effectiveness of other students' work.

Independent Practice Use the On Your Own activity (page 34) as homework or review. Encourage students to use what they learned in the lesson to complete the assignment. Tell students they can choose a recipe from the Idea Box or think of one of their own.

Name _____ Date _____

A Smoothie

How do you make a smoothie?

- Introduce the topic.
- Focus on your writing purpose and audience.
- List the ingredients and steps.
- Organize the steps in order.
- Use transition words.
- On another sheet of paper, explain how to make a smoothie.

1 c. orange juice
1 c. raspberries
6 oz. plain yogurt
1 peach, cut up
1 tbsp. honey
2–3 ice cubes

Topic _____

Writing Purpose _____

Audience _____

Ingredients _____

_____

_____

_____

Steps in Order _____

_____

_____

_____

_____

_____

_____

Possible Transition Words _____

_____

Name _____ Date _____

On Your Own

Choose a recipe to make from the Idea Box or think of one of your own. Research your topic to complete the page. On another sheet of paper, explain how to make the food.

Idea Box

- ○ French Toast   ○ Granola   ○ Grilled Cheese Sandwich
- ○ My Idea: _____

Topic _____

Writing Purpose _____

Audience _____

Ingredients _____

_____

_____

_____

Steps in Order _____

_____

_____

_____

_____

_____

_____

_____

Possible Transition Words _____

_____

Writing Lessons to Meet the Common Core: Grade 6 © 2013 by Linda Ward Beech, Scholastic Teaching Resources

Informative Writing
Caves

Introduction Provide each student with a copy of the writing frame (page 36). Have students read the title and first line. Tell students they will write an informative text about caves. Their audience will be other class members. Remind students that the purpose of informative writing is to educate the reader and usually requires research. Assemble appropriate reference materials and a computer with Internet access. Students will also need to use these during the Independent Practice activity.

Model Suggest a sentence to introduce the topic. For example:

* Beneath the surface of Earth are hollow areas called caves.

Help students identify information to develop the topic. For example:

* dark, no sun, tunnels, chambers
* often underground rivers, lakes
* formed in limestone
* surface water seeps into cracks, dissolves rock
* speleology is study of caves
* thousands of years

Coach students in developing the information into complete sentences and organizing it for clarity. The first two sentences below tell what a cave is like and the next three sentences tell how caves are formed. The last sentence gives additional information about caves. Point out that you will be using words specific to geology and speleology (the study of caves) such as *sedimentary* and *limestone*. For example:

* Caves are dark, damp underground rooms and passages that receive no sunlight. Caves often have rivers, lakes, and even waterfalls.
* Caves are usually formed in a sedimentary rock called limestone. Water from the surface seeps into the layers of this rock and slowly dissolves it making tunnels and chambers. This process takes thousands of years.
* The study of caves is called speleology.

Tell students that it is useful to include an illustration or graphic representation to help readers. Have them research and draw a cross-section of a cave for this paper.

Guided Practice Have students complete the writing frame. Encourage them to use their own research, wording, and sentence structure.

Review Call on volunteers to read their finished pieces to the class. Have listeners use items 1, 2, 4, 5, 8–10, and 13 on the assessment checklist (page 63) to evaluate the effectiveness of other students' work.

Independent Practice Use the On Your Own activity (page 31) as homework or review. Encourage students to use what they know about taking notes (see Lesson 7) when researching and writing an informative text. Explain that students can choose a cave topic from the Idea Box or use one of their own. Remind them to use reliable sources and relevant facts for their research.

Caves

What is a cave?

- Introduce the topic.
- Focus on your writing purpose and audience.
- Develop the topic with researched facts and science words.
- Organize the information.
- On another sheet of paper, write an informative text about caves.
- Include an illustration showing a cross-section of a cave.

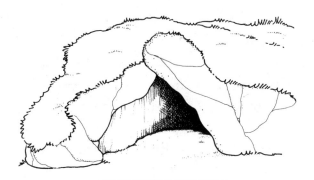

Some people call a cave a cavern.

Topic _____

Writing Purpose _____

Audience _____

Facts _____

_____

_____

_____

Possible Science Words _____

Organizing Information

Group 1 _____

_____

_____

Group 2 _____

_____

_____

Group 3 _____

Name _____ Date _____

On Your Own

Choose another aspect of caves from the Idea Box or think of one of your own. Research your topic to complete the page. Then, write an informative text on another sheet of paper. Include an illustration.

Idea Box

○ Cave Dwellers   ○ Spelunking   ○ Formations in Caves

○ My Idea: _____

Topic _____

Writing Purpose _____

Audience _____

Facts _____

_____

_____

_____

Possible Science Words _____

Organizing Information

Group 1 _____

_____

_____

Group 2 _____

_____

_____

Group 3 _____

Informative Writing
Sharks

Objectives & Common Core Connections

* Introduce the topic for a selected audience.
* Focus on the purpose of informative writing.
* Develop the topic with researched, relevant facts.
* Use precise language.
* Organize information to compare and contrast.
* Write an informative text in a formal style.

Introduction Provide each student with a copy of the writing frame (page 39). Have students read the title and first line. Tell students they will write an informative text comparing two kinds of sharks. Their audience will be readers of a science journal the class is compiling. Remind students that this kind of informative writing will require research. Assemble appropriate reference materials and a computer with Internet access. Students will also need to use these during the Independent Practice activity.

Model Tell students that you will use a formal writing style for this audience. Say: *In a formal style, you avoid contractions, abbreviations, and slang. You write in the third person, and your tone is polite but impersonal.* Point out that a formal style is usually used in science journals. Suggest a sentence to introduce the topic. For example:

* Two of the largest fish in the ocean are the great white shark and the shortfin mako shark.

Help students identify information to develop the topic. For example:

* great white—21' long; about 5,000 pounds; powerful swimmer; dangerous predator; attacks fishing boats and people; eats tuna, sea lions, elephant seals, other sharks

* mako—10' long; about 1,000 pounds; fastest swimmer; capable of attacking boats and people; eats fish such as mackerel, bonito, swordfish, also sea birds, turtles; prized as game fish

Coach students in developing the information into complete sentences and organizing it to compare and contrast the sharks. Point out that you are using precise language, such as *dangerous predator*. For example:

* The great white shark measures up to 21 feet and weighs about 5,000 pounds. It is a powerful swimmer and a dangerous predator. The white shark is known to have attacked fishing boats and people. For its normal diet, this shark hunts large animals such as sea lions, elephant seals, and other sharks.

* At 10 feet long and 1,000 pounds, the shortfin mako shark is shorter and lighter than the great white shark. It is the fastest known shark and can be potentially dangerous to people. The mako eats fish such as mackerel, bonito, and swordfish as well as sea birds and turtles.

Guided Practice Have students complete the writing frame. Encourage them to use their own research, wording, and sentence structure.

Review Call on volunteers to read their finished pieces to the class. Have listeners use items 1, 2, 4, 5, 9–11, and 13 on the assessment checklist (page 63) to evaluate the effectiveness of other students' work.

Independent Practice Use the On Your Own activity (page 40) as homework or review. Encourage students to use what they know about taking notes (see Lesson 7) when researching and writing an informative text. Explain that students can choose animals to compare from the Idea Box or use their own idea. Remind them to use reliable sources and relevant facts for their research.

Sharks

How are these sharks alike and different?

- Introduce the topic.
- Focus on your writing purpose and audience.
- Develop the topic with researched facts and precise language.
- Organize the information to compare and contrast.
- On another sheet of paper, write an informative text in a formal style.

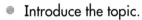

mako shark

great white shark

Topic _____

Writing Purpose _____

Audience _____

Facts _____

_____

_____

_____

_____

Precise Words _____

Organizing Information

Great White Shark _____

_____

_____

_____

Mako Shark _____

_____

_____

On Your Own

Choose two types of an animal from the Idea Box or think of your own idea. Research your topic to complete the page. On another sheet of paper, write an informative text in a formal style.

Idea Box

○ Two Kinds of Elephants

○ Two Kinds of Whales

○ Two Kinds of Bears

○ My Idea: _____

_____

_____

Topic _____

Writing Purpose _____

Audience _____

Facts _____

_____

_____

_____

_____

Precise Words _____

Organizing Information

Type 1 _____

_____

_____

_____

Type 2 _____

_____

_____

_____

Informative Writing
A National Park

Objectives & Common Core Connections

* Introduce the topic.
* Focus on the writing purpose and audience.
* Develop the text by using researched facts and quotations and organizing the information.
* Write a concluding sentence and include a graphic.
* Write an informative text in a formal style.

Introduction Provide each student with a copy of the writing frame (page 42). Have students read the title and first line. Tell students they will write an informative report about Sequoia National Park for a social studies class. Assemble appropriate reference materials and a computer with Internet access. Students will also need to use these during the Independent Practice activity.

Model Tell students that they will use a formal writing style. Say: *In a formal style, you avoid contractions, abbreviations, and slang. You write in the third person, and your tone is polite but impersonal.* Suggest a sentence to introduce the topic. For example:

* Sequoia National Park, a region of spectacular natural resources, is located in the Sierra Nevada mountain range near Visalia, California.

Help students identify information from their research to develop the topic. For example:

* established in 1890; John Muir
* mountains, canyons, caves, wildlife
* camping, hiking, fishing
* Tunnel Log
* famous for giant sequoias, General Sherman Tree
* 404,063 acres dramatic wilderness with trails but few roads

Coach students in organizing the information and developing it into complete sentences. The first group of sentences below tells about the park, and the second group tells what people do there.

* The park was established in 1890 with the help of John Muir (1838–1914), a well-known naturalist and a forceful proponent of creating national parks for everyone to enjoy. The park's name comes from the giant sequoia forests it encompasses. Many of these are 250-feet tall and have a diameter of 20 feet. One sequoia, the General Sherman, is considered the world's largest tree. Within the park's 404,063 acres are high mountain peaks, deep canyons, hundreds of caves, vast areas of wilderness, and diverse wildlife.

* Visitors enjoy hiking, camping, and fishing. They also like driving through the Tunnel Log, created from a fallen sequoia.

Explain that a report should have a concluding statement to restate the main point. In this case the statement is a quotation. Ask students to include a map of the park with their reports.

* Said John Muir of the lands he sought to preserve, "In every walk with Nature one receives far more than he seeks."

Guided Practice Have students complete the writing frame. Encourage them to use their own research, wording, and sentence structure.

Review Call on volunteers to read their finished reports. Have listeners use items 1, 2, 4, 5, 8, 9, and 11–13 on the assessment checklist (page 63) to evaluate the effectiveness of other students' work.

Independent Practice Use the On Your Own activity (page 43) as homework or review. Remind students to use what they know about taking notes (see Lesson 7) when researching and writing an informative text. Students can choose a national park from the Idea Box or think of one of their own.

A National Park

What is Sequoia National Park like?

- Introduce the topic.
- Focus on your writing purpose and audience.
- Develop the topic with researched facts and quotations.
- Organize the information.
- Write a concluding sentence and include a map.
- On another sheet of paper, write a report about Sequoia National Park.

Topic _____

Writing Purpose _____

Audience _____

Facts _____

_____

_____

_____

Quotation _____

_____

Organizing Information

Group 1 _____

_____

_____

Group 2 _____

_____

_____

Concluding Statement _____

_____

Name _____ Date _____

On Your Own

Choose a national park from the Idea Box or think of one of your own. Research your topic to complete the page. On another sheet of paper, write a report about the park. Include a map.

Idea Box

○ Yellowstone

○ Acadia

○ Great Smoky Mountains

○ My Idea: _____

_____

_____

Topic _____

Writing Purpose _____

Audience _____

Facts _____

_____

_____

_____

Quotation _____

_____

Organizing Information

Group 1 _____

_____

_____

Group 2 _____

_____

_____

Concluding Statement _____

_____

Narrative Writing
Bike Adventure

Objectives & Common Core Connections

* Focus on the writing purpose.
* Develop an imaginary situation or experience.
* Establish characters.
* Write a strong opening sentence.

Introduction Provide each student with a copy of the writing frame (page 45). Have students read the title and first lines. Ask students to explain what story they think the illustration suggests. Tell them that they will develop ideas for a narrative based on the picture. Remind students that a narrative is a story or account of something and is written to entertain readers.

Model Say: *I'm going to brainstorm what else the illustration suggests.* For example:

* neighborhood street
* boy is careless
* bike feels neglected
* bike looking for adventure
* boy running after bike

Mention that you are going to give the boy in the illustration a name. Guide students in developing the situation and the characters of the bike and the boy. Remind students that this is an imaginary experience. For example:

* Jesse often leaves his bike out overnight even when it rains. He recently has been hanging out with his friends and ignoring the bike. Jesse is careless with his belongings, interested in having fun, and not too responsible.

* The bike is tired of lying on the lawn and getting wet. The bike's feelings are hurt because Jesse has been ignoring it, so it decides to go off on an adventure by itself. The bike is sensitive and has an independent streak.

Point out that a story needs a good beginning to draw in readers. Provide an introductory sentence related to the illustration. For example:

* Jesse was stunned when he saw his bike riding down the street without him—or anyone else—on it.

Guided Practice Have students complete the writing frame. Encourage them to use their own ideas about the situation and characters. Guide students in developing the story further by asking questions such as: *Does the bike succeed in having some good adventures? Is Jesse able to catch the bike? What happens when other people see the riderless bike? Do Jesse and the bike resolve their differences?* Suggest that students develop a narrative about the characters and situation on another sheet of paper.

Review Invite volunteers to share their finished pages with the class. Have listeners use items 1 and 3–5 on the assessment checklist (page 64) to evaluate other student's work.

Independent Practice Use the On Your Own activity (page 46) as homework or review. Encourage students to use what they learned in the lesson to complete the assignment. Tell students they can choose a story topic from the Idea Box or think of one of their own.

Writing Lessons to Meet the Common Core: Grade 6 © 2013 by Linda Ward Beech, Scholastic Teaching Resources

Name _____ Date _____

Bike Adventure

What happens when a bike goes for a ride by itself? Use the illustration to tell a story.

- Focus on your writing purpose.
- Tell what the situation is.
- Tell who the characters are.
- Write a strong opening sentence.

Writing Purpose _____

_____

Situation _____

_____

_____

_____

_____

Character 1 _____

_____

_____

_____

Character 2 _____

_____

_____

_____

Opening Sentence _____

_____

On Your Own

Choose a story topic from the Idea Box or think of one of your own.
Complete this page to develop your narrative.

Idea Box

○ Cell Phone That Calls Your Friends to Talk

○ TV That Wants to Watch Its Favorite Programs

○ Video Game That Won't Let You Win

○ My Idea: _____

_____

Writing Purpose _____

_____

Situation _____

_____

_____

_____

Character 1 _____

_____

_____

_____

Character 2 _____

_____

_____

_____

Opening Sentence _____

_____

Narrative Writing
Backwards Day

Objectives & Common Core Connections

* Focus on writing purpose for a selected audience.
* Develop an imaginary situation or experience.
* Establish a character.
* Write a strong opening sentence.
* Organize events in order.
* Write a narrative.

Introduction Provide each student with a copy of the writing frame (page 48). Discuss the title and question. Tell students they will write a narrative for other sixth graders. Review that a narrative is a story or account of something and is written to entertain. A narrative can be about something imaginary or real.

Model Say: *I'm going to brainstorm what a backwards day might be like.* For example:

* reverse order of events
* confusion for character
* starts with a girl's wish
* relief when it ends
* no more wishes

Tell students you are going to give the girl a name, *Sally.* Model how to develop the situation into a narrative. Review that a narrative should have a beginning, middle, and end. Suggest a beginning sentence. For example:

* Sally would never forget the day when time went backwards.

Work with students to organize the events in a backwards sequence and to develop complete sentences. For example:

It all began with a silly wish. Sally wished that when she woke up in the morning, it would really be evening and she could watch TV. Sure enough, her wish came true, and Sally found herself watching her favorite nighttime program the next morning. After that, she ate supper and did her homework. Next, she went to after school sports. She got a B+ on the social studies test during the last period of school. Mrs. Wolf assigned a book report during English that afternoon, and the class did experiments in science. At least lunch took place at about the same time as usual. Sally yawned a few times in her morning classes, but managed to review for the social studies test during a study period. By the time she got on the bus to go home for breakfast, her head was spinning. Just before she went to bed, Sally made another wish—that things would go back to normal by the next day. After that, Sally didn't think she would make any more wishes.

Guided Practice Have students complete the writing frame. Encourage them to use their own ideas about the situation and character.

Review Invite volunteers to share their finished narratives with the class. Have listeners use items 1–6 and 12 on the assessment checklist (page 64) to evaluate the effectiveness of other students' work.

Independent Practice Use the On Your Own activity (page 49) as homework or review. Encourage students to use what they learned in the lesson to complete the assignment. Tell students to choose a topic from the Idea Box or think of one of their own.

Backwards Day

What would a backwards day be like?

- Focus on your writing purpose, keeping your audience in mind.
- Develop the situation and character.
- Write a strong opening sentence.
- Organize the events in order.
- Write your narrative on another sheet of paper.

Good Night.

Good Morning.

Writing Purpose _____

_____

Audience _____

Situation _____

_____

_____

Character _____

_____

Opening Sentence _____

_____

Order of Events _____

_____

_____

_____

_____

_____

Name _____ Date _____

On Your Own

Choose a story topic from the Idea Box or think of one of your own.
Complete this page. Then, write your narrative on another sheet of paper.

Idea Box

○ Day in the Future   ○ My Idea: _____

○ Day in Space   _____

○ Day in the Past   _____

Writing Purpose _____

_____

Audience _____

Situation _____

_____

_____

Character _____

_____

Opening Sentence _____

_____

Order of Events _____

_____

_____

_____

_____

_____

Narrative Writing
Dad's Dinner

Objectives & Common Core Connections

* Focus on writing purpose for a selected audience.
* Develop characters and a situation or experience.
* Write a strong opening sentence.
* Use dialogue.
* Organize the events in order.
* Write a narrative.

Introduction Provide each student with a copy of the writing frame (page 51). Discuss the title and first line. Tell students they will write a narrative for elementary school students. Review that a narrative is a story or account of something and is written to entertain.

Model Summarize the situation in the illustrations and discuss the characters, a father and daughter. Model a sentence to begin the narrative. For example:

* Anita's dad was always trying new recipes; Anita never knew what to expect.

Coach students in describing what the pictures show. For example:

* father has new chicken recipe
* father forgets chicken
* daughter is skeptical
* daughter says they'll eat cereal for supper
* father shops for long list of ingredients

Work with students to organize the events and develop complete sentences about them. For example:

* One morning Dad announced that he had a great new chicken recipe he was going to make for dinner that night. Anita was dubious; she had eaten Dad's new recipes before. Dad wrote out a long list of ingredients to buy and headed out to the store.

Draw attention to the speech balloons in the illustrations and point out that a writer uses dialogue to show how a character feels and responds to an event. For example:

* "This recipe sure has a lot of ingredients," said Dad as he emptied his grocery bags.

* Anita watched as he filled the counter with food. Finally, she asked, "Where's the chicken?"

* Dad's face fell as he realized he had forgotten the main ingredient. Then he and Anita began to laugh. "Cereal tonight!" she said giving him a big grin.

Guided Practice Have students complete the writing frame. Encourage them to use their own interpretations about the situation and characters and their own dialogue if they wish.

Review Invite volunteers to share their finished narratives with the class. Have listeners use items 1–7 and 12 on the assessment checklist (page 64) to evaluate the effectiveness of other students' work.

Independent Practice Use the On Your Own activity (page 52) as homework or review. Encourage students to use what they learned in the lesson to complete the assignment. Tell students they can choose a topic from the Idea Box or think of one of their own.

Dad's Dinner Use the illustrations to write a narrative.

- Focus on your writing purpose, keeping your audience in mind.
- Develop the situation and characters.
- Write a strong opening sentence.
- Organize the events in order.
- Use dialogue.
- Write your narrative on another sheet of paper.

Writing Purpose _____

Audience _____

Situation _____

_____

_____

Character 1 _____

Character 2 _____

Opening Sentence _____

_____

Order of Events _____

_____

_____

Dialogue _____

_____

Name _____ Date _____

On Your Own

Choose a story topic from the Idea Box or think of one of your own.
Complete this page. Then, write your narrative on another sheet of paper.

Idea Box

○ Forgotten Umbrella

○ Forgotten Gift

○ Forgotten Gloves

○ My Idea: _____

_____

_____

Writing Purpose _____

Audience _____

Situation _____

_____

_____

Character 1 _____

Character 2 _____

Opening Sentence _____

_____

Order of Events _____

_____

_____

Dialogue _____

_____

_____

_____

Narrative Writing
Mystery Excursion

Objectives & Common Core Connections

* Focus on writing purpose for a selected audience.
* Develop characters and a situation or experience.
* Write a strong opening sentence.
* Use transition words, phrases, and clauses.
* Organize the events in order.
* Write a first-person narrative.

Introduction Provide each student with a copy of the writing frame (page 54). Discuss the title and first line. Tell students they will write a first-person narrative for a school literary journal. Their readers will be other students, parents, and teachers. Remind students that a first-person narrative uses the pronoun *I* and is told from the writer's point of view.

Model Summarize the situation in the illustrations and identify the characters as a grandfather and grandson. Explain that the *I* in this narrative will be the boy and *we* will be the boy and his grandfather. Model a sentence to begin the narrative. For example:

* My grandfather loved to take me on what he called "mystery excursions."

Coach students in describing what the picture suggests. Point out that you are using your imagination to add more details. For example:

* in pickup truck
* donating pots and pans
* at a swap shop at a town dump
* boy looking dubious
* finding a soccer ball and fishing rod
* unusual destinations

Work with students to organize the events and develop complete sentences about them. Model how transition words, phrases, and clauses, such as *before* and *by the time*, can help convey sequence and signal shifts from one setting to another. For example:

* His destinations were offbeat and usually quite interesting. For example, instead of going to see a circus performance, we would go to see the circus being set up.

* Before a recent excursion, Grandfather loaded a box of pots and pans into his pickup truck. I knew better than to ask about them; it was an unwritten rule that the excursions were a surprise. We drove along some winding roads at the outskirts of town until we came to the town dump. I WAS surprised. What kind of a destination was a dump?

* Still, I said nothing. Grandfather stopped at a small building labeled "Swap Shop" and hauled out his pots and pans. He deposited these in the Swap Shop and then began looking around. I joined him and soon discovered a practically new soccer ball. Grandfather scored a fishing rod in great condition. By the time we left, we were both the proud owners of nifty swapped "treasures"!

Guided Practice Have students complete the writing frame. Encourage them to use their own dialogue and details to show how the characters respond to the events.

Review Invite volunteers to share their finished narratives with the class Have listeners use items 1–6, 10, and 12 on the assessment checklist (page 64) to evaluate the effectiveness of other students' work.

Independent Practice Use the On Your Own activity (page 55) as homework or review. Tell students they can choose a topic from the Idea Box or use one of their own.

Name _____ Date _____

Mystery Excursions

⭐ What is a mystery excursion?

- Focus on your writing purpose, keeping your audience in mind.
- Develop the situation and characters.
- Write a strong opening sentence.
- Organize the events in order using transition words, phrases, or clauses.
- Write a first-person narrative on another sheet of paper.

Writing Purpose _____

Audience _____

Situation _____

_____

_____

Character 1 _____

Character 2 _____

Opening Sentence _____

_____

Order of Events _____

_____

_____

_____

_____

Transition Words _____

_____

Name _____ Date _____

On Your Own

Choose a mystery excursion from the Idea Box or think of one of your own. Complete this page. Then, write your first-person narrative on another sheet of paper.

Idea Box

○ Backstage of Theater

○ Skateboard Factory

○ Warehouse Distribution Center

○ My Idea: _____

_____

_____

Writing Purpose _____

Audience _____

Situation _____

_____

_____

Character 1 _____

Character 2 _____

Opening Sentence _____

_____

Order of Events _____

_____

_____

_____

_____

Transition Words _____

_____

Narrative Writing
State Fair

Objectives & Common Core Connections

* Focus on writing purpose for a selected audience.
* Develop characters and a situation or experience.
* Write a strong opening sentence.
* Use sensory words and description.
* Organize the events in order.
* Write a descriptive narrative.

Introduction Provide each student with a copy of the writing frame (page 57). Discuss the title and first line. Tell students they will write a descriptive narrative about a visit to a state fair. Their audience will be students who have never been to a fair.

Model Draw attention to the illustration and explain that you will use your imagination to create two characters and a narrative. Model a sentence to begin the narrative. For example:

* Before they even parked the car, Tanya and her aunt were caught up in the excitement of the State Fair.

Coach students in using the illustration to develop descriptive elements for the narrative. For example:

* hot dogs, popcorn, ice cream
* thrilling rides
* farm animals and barnyard smells
* music, dancing, contests
* huge crowds
* farm goods

Work with students to organize the material and develop complete sentences. Explain that you want to use sensory words and phrases to capture the sights, sounds, smells, tastes, and feelings of the fair. For example:

* As they made their way to the barns full of animals, Tanya sniffed the sweet smell of hay. Inside, large cows chewed quietly while their owners showed off proudly won ribbons. In another barn, Tanya gently stroked the soft wool of a lamb while some nearby goats bleated and boldly tried to eat her sleeve. Farther along, they passed rows of pies, jams, cakes, and other homemade goods. They admired giant pumpkins, squash, melons, and sunflowers that farmers grew.

The twangs of a country band greeted Tanya and Aunt Lucy when they stepped outside. Many people danced and clapped to the music. A log-pulling contest caught Tanya's eye, and the tempting aromas of hot dogs, popcorn, and giant waffles got the attention of her stomach. Aunt Lucy bought her a grilled bratwurst. Everywhere there were throngs of people eating, talking, buying souvenirs, and hurrying to the next attraction.

Tanya and Aunt Lucy ended their visit with a ride on the Ferris Wheel. It was dizzying and grand!

Guided Practice Have students complete the writing frame. Encourage students to use their own ideas of what a state fair would be like.

Review Invite volunteers to share their finished narratives with the class. Have students use items 1–6, 8–9, and 12 on the assessment checklist (page 64) to evaluate the effectiveness of other students' work.

Independent Practice Use the On Your Own activity (page 58) as homework or review. Tell students they can choose a topic from the Idea Box or use one of their own.

Name _____   Date _____

State Fair

What is a state fair like?

- Focus on your writing purpose, keeping your audience in mind.
- Develop the characters and situation.
- Write a strong opening sentence.
- Organize the events in order.
- Use sensory words.
- Write your descriptive narrative on another sheet of paper.

Writing Purpose _____

Audience _____

Situation _____

_____

_____

Character 1 _____

Character 2 _____

Opening Sentence _____

_____

Order of Events _____

_____

_____

_____

_____

Sensory Words _____

_____

On Your Own

Choose an event from the Idea Box or think of one of your own. Complete this page. Then, write your descriptive narrative on another sheet of paper.

Idea Box

○ Automobile Race   ○ My Idea: _____

○ Professional Ball Game   _____

○ Celebratory Parade   _____

Writing Purpose _____

Audience _____

Situation _____

_____

_____

Character 1 _____

Character 2 _____

Opening Sentence _____

_____

Order of Events _____

_____

_____

_____

_____

_____

Sensory Words _____

_____

Narrative Writing
Treasure Hunt

Objectives & Common Core Connections

* Focus on writing purpose for a selected audience.
* Develop characters and a situation or experience.
* Write a strong opening and concluding sentence.
* Use dialogue and transitional words.
* Organize the events in order.
* Write a narrative.

Introduction Provide each student with a copy of the writing frame (page 60). Discuss the title and first line. Tell students they will write a narrative about how a boy helps his sister improve her math skills. Their audience will be students in fourth grade.

Model Draw attention to the illustration and explain that you will use your imagination to create two characters and a narrative. Point out that you are naming the characters *Jackson* and *Lark*. Model sentences to begin the narrative. For example:

* Jackson's little sister loved to read; she read all the time. Her favorite books were about treasure hunts. The problem was Lark even read in math class.

Coach students in using the illustration to develop a narrative. For example:

* Lark needs help
* treasure hunt with math clues
* book about treasure hunts
* Jackson has idea
* Lark solves clues
* skills improve

Work with students to organize the material so it has a beginning, middle, and end. Point out that

you will use dialogue and transitional words to convey the content and sequence of the narrative. For example:

* One day, Lark brought home a note from school about her mediocre math skills. Jackson had an idea.

  "How would you like to go on your own treasure hunt?" he asked. Lark looked up from the book she was reading. "Will there really be a treasure?" she asked. Jackson nodded, then set to work. He wrote 10 clues on index cards. Each clue was a math problem. Then Jackson went to the store and returned with a package wrapped in paper. The next day, he set up the treasure hunt, placing the cards around the house. Then he called Lark and gave her the first clue: "Start at the kitchen table facing the door. Take 3 x 4 steps."

  Lark glared at him as she worked out the problem. "You do want to find the treasure, right?" said Jackson. Finally, Lark reached clue #10 and the treasure.

Point out that a narrative has an ending or conclusion. For example:

* She had sharpened her math skills and won a book about treasure hunts as well!

Guided Practice Have students complete the writing frame. Encourage them to use their own dialogue, details, and ending.

Review Invite volunteers to share their finished narratives with the class. Have students use items 1–7 and 10–12 on the assessment checklist (page 64) to evaluate the effectiveness of other students' work.

Independent Practice Use the On Your Own activity (page 61) as homework or review. Tell students they can choose a topic from the Idea Box or think of one of their own.

Name _____ Date _____

Treasure Hunt

Use the illustration to write a narrative.

- Focus on your writing purpose, keeping your audience in mind.
- Develop the characters and situation.
- Write a strong opening and closing sentence.
- Organize the events in order.
- Use transitional words and dialogue.
- Write your narrative on another sheet of paper.

Writing Purpose _____

Audience _____

Situation _____

_____

_____

Character 1 _____

Character 2 _____

Opening Sentence _____

_____

Order of Events _____

_____

_____

_____

Dialogue _____

_____

_____

Transitional Words _____

Ending Sentence _____

_____

Name _____ Date _____

On Your Own

Choose a topic from the Idea Box or think of one of your own. Complete this page. Then, write your narrative on another sheet of paper.

Idea Box

○ Helping a Poor Speller   ○ My Idea: _____

○ Coaching a Slow Runner   _____

○ Building a Student's Vocabulary   _____

Writing Purpose _____

Audience _____

Situation _____

_____

_____

Character 1 _____

Character 2 _____

Opening Sentence _____

_____

Order of Events _____

_____

_____

_____

Dialogue _____

_____

Transitional Words _____

Ending Sentence _____

Student Assessment Checklist
Argument Writing

1. Introduced a claim. .... ☐

2. Focused on the writing purpose. .... ☐

3. Supported claim with clear reasons, relevant evidence, and reliable sources. .... ☐

4. Organized reasons/evidence clearly. .... ☐

5. Addressed the audience appropriately. .... ☐

6. Used words, phrases, or clauses to clarify relationships among claim and reasons. .... ☐

7. Established a formal style. .... ☐

8. Provided a concluding statement. .... ☐

9. Wrote an argument. .... ☐

More Things to Check

● Capitalized proper nouns. ☐

● Capitalized the first word of sentences. ☐

● Used correct punctuation. ☐

● Spelled words correctly. ☐

● Followed correct paragraph form. ☐

Writing Lessons to Meet the Common Core: Grade 6 © 2013 by Linda Ward Beech, Scholastic Teaching Resources

Name _____ Date _____

Student Assessment Checklist
Informative/Explanatory Writing

1. Introduced the topic. .... ☐

2. Focused on the writing purpose. .... ☐

3. Summarized and paraphrased the information in notes. .... ☐

4. Developed the topic using credible sources to research relevant
facts, definitions, details, quotations, and examples. .... ☐

5. Organized the information using strategies such as definition,
compare/contrast, and cause/effect. .... ☐

6. Used transitions to clarify relationships. .... ☐

7. Listed materials and steps for a how-to piece. .... ☐

8. Included a graphic to aid comprehension. .... ☐

9. Addressed the audience appropriately. .... ☐

10. Used subject-specific words and precise language. .... ☐

11. Used a formal style. .... ☐

12. Included a concluding sentence. .... ☐

13. Wrote an informative/explanatory piece. .... ☐

More Things to Check

● Capitalized proper nouns. ☐

● Capitalized the first word of sentences. ☐

● Used correct punctuation. ☐

● Spelled words correctly. ☐

● Followed correct paragraph form. ☐

Writing Lessons to Meet the Common Core: Grade 6 © 2013 by Linda Ward Beech, Scholastic Teaching Resources

Name _____ Date _____

Student Assessment Checklist
Narrative Writing

1. Focused on the writing purpose. .... ☐

2. Addressed the audience appropriately. .... ☐

3. Developed a real or imaginary experience or event. .... ☐

4. Established characters and/or a narrator. .... ☐

5. Provided a strong opening. .... ☐

6. Organized the sequence of events. .... ☐

7. Included dialogue. .... ☐

8. Used description. .... ☐

9. Used sensory language and precise words and phrases. .... ☐

10. Used transitional words. .... ☐

11. Provided a conclusion. .... ☐

12. Wrote a narrative. .... ☐

More Things to Check

● Capitalized proper nouns. ☐

● Capitalized the first word of sentences. ☐

● Used correct punctuation. ☐

● Spelled words correctly. ☐

● Followed correct paragraph form. ☐

Writing Lessons to Meet the Common Core: Grade 6 © 2013 by Linda Ward Beech, Scholastic Teaching Resources